TABLE OF CONTENTS

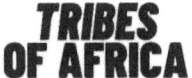

LET'S BEGIN

Welcome to "Tribes of Africa: Women's Edition," where each stroke of your pencil celebrates the strength and spirit of Africa's women. This coloring book is a tribute to the hardworking mothers, sisters, wives, grandmothers, and daughters who are the backbone of their communities.

As you explore these pages, you'll encounter the diverse roles and immense contributions of African women, from nurturing families to preserving centuries-old traditions.

Through the art of coloring, you'll connect with stories of resilience, love, and wisdom that these women embody. Every image here highlights their importance in shaping not only their families but also the cultural and social landscapes of Africa. Their hands weave the fabric of their tribes' heritage, their voices tell

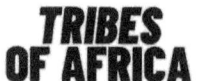

the tales of generations, and their resilience drives the future.

In coloring their portraits, you're honoring the legacy and celebrating the enduring influence of African women. May this book deepen your appreciation for the pivotal role they play in the tapestry of African life and inspire admiration for their unyielding strength and grace. Let's color in honor of these remarkable women, the unsung heroines of Africa. We love you and thank you.

Special Thanks

Grace Naa Brown
Zaza
Bella
Kare

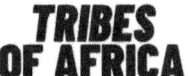

AMHARA

(am·haa·ruh)

The Amhara are a group of people who live far away in the country of Ethiopia in Africa.

They have lived in Ethiopia for hundreds and hundreds of years.

The Amhara speak their own language called Amharic.

They have their own cultural traditions, food, music, and clothes.

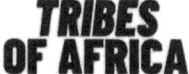

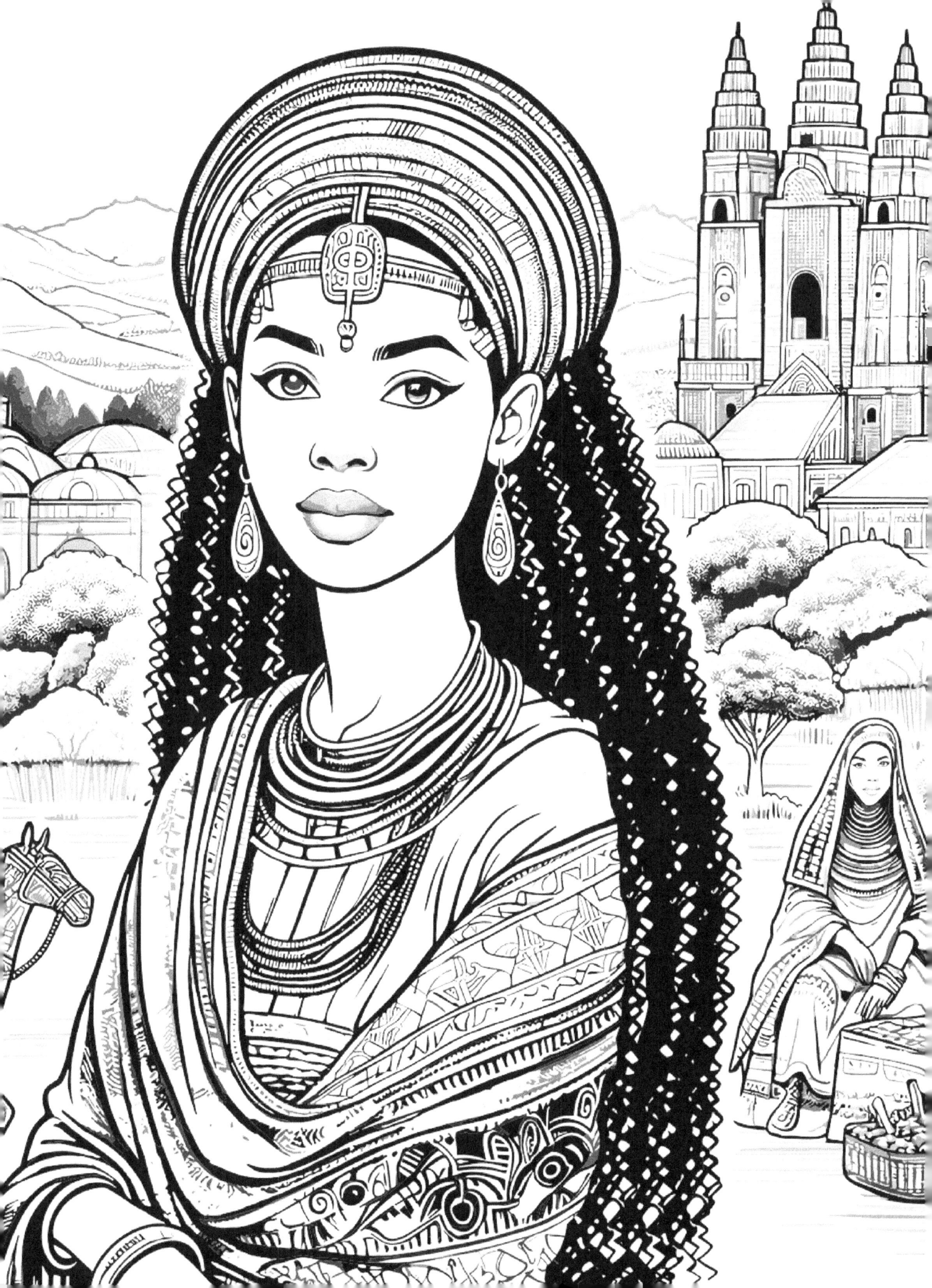

ASHANTI
(uh·shaan·tee)

The Ashanti people live in the country of Ghana in West Africa.

They have lived in central Ghana for hundreds of years.

The Ashanti speak their own language called Twi.

In the past, the Ashanti had a powerful empire ruled by their king, the Asantehene.

The Ashanti were great warriors who fought many battles using spears and shields.

They also mined gold and traded it with Europeans who came on ships.

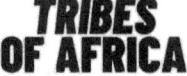

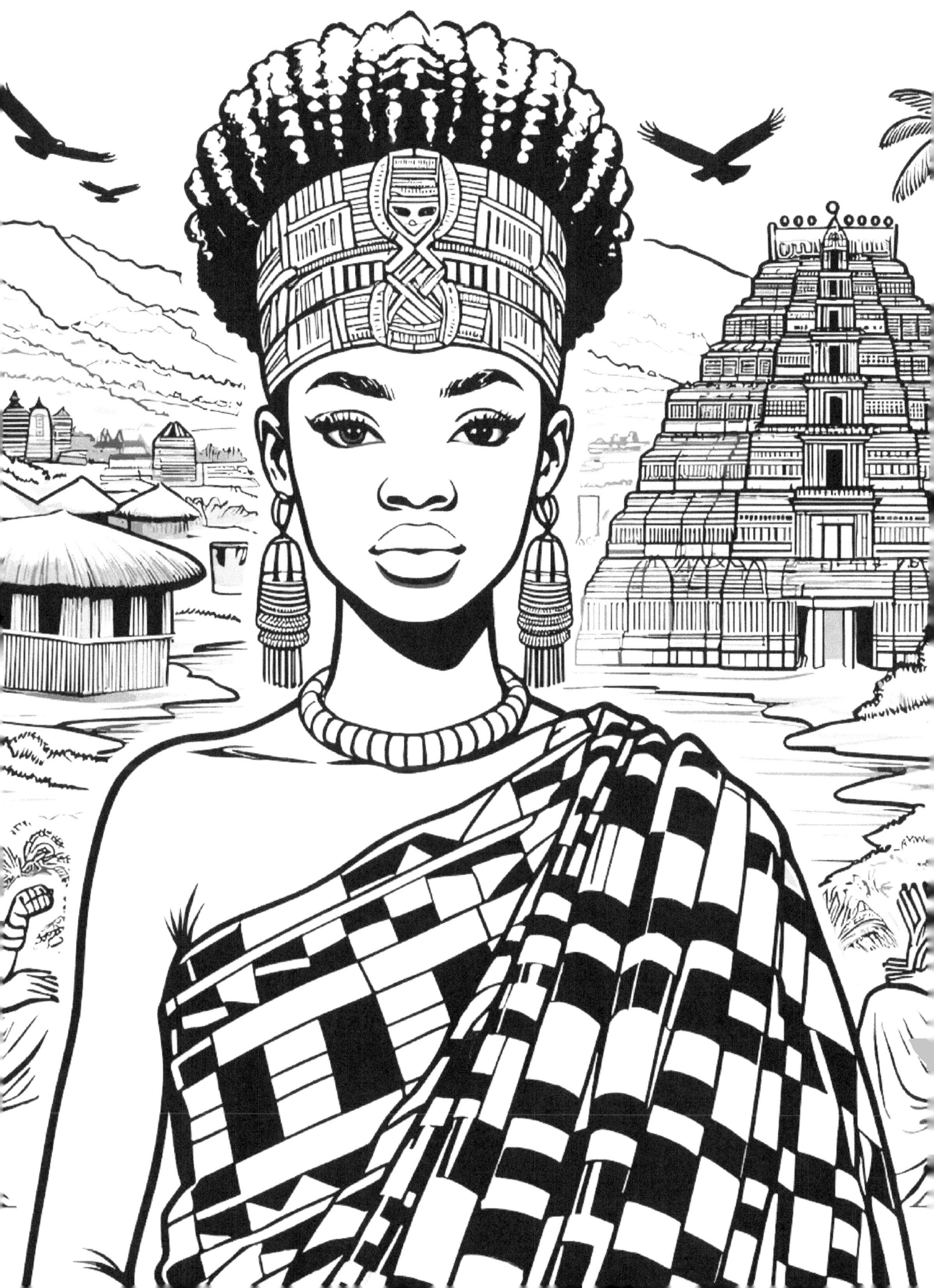

BEMBA
(bem·buh)

The Bemba are a group of people who live in the country of Zambia in Africa.

They have lived there for hundreds of years.

The Bemba speak their own language called Chibemba.

Long ago, they had their own Bemba kingdom and their own king called Chitimukulu.

The Bemba used to be warriors and farmers.

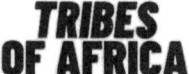

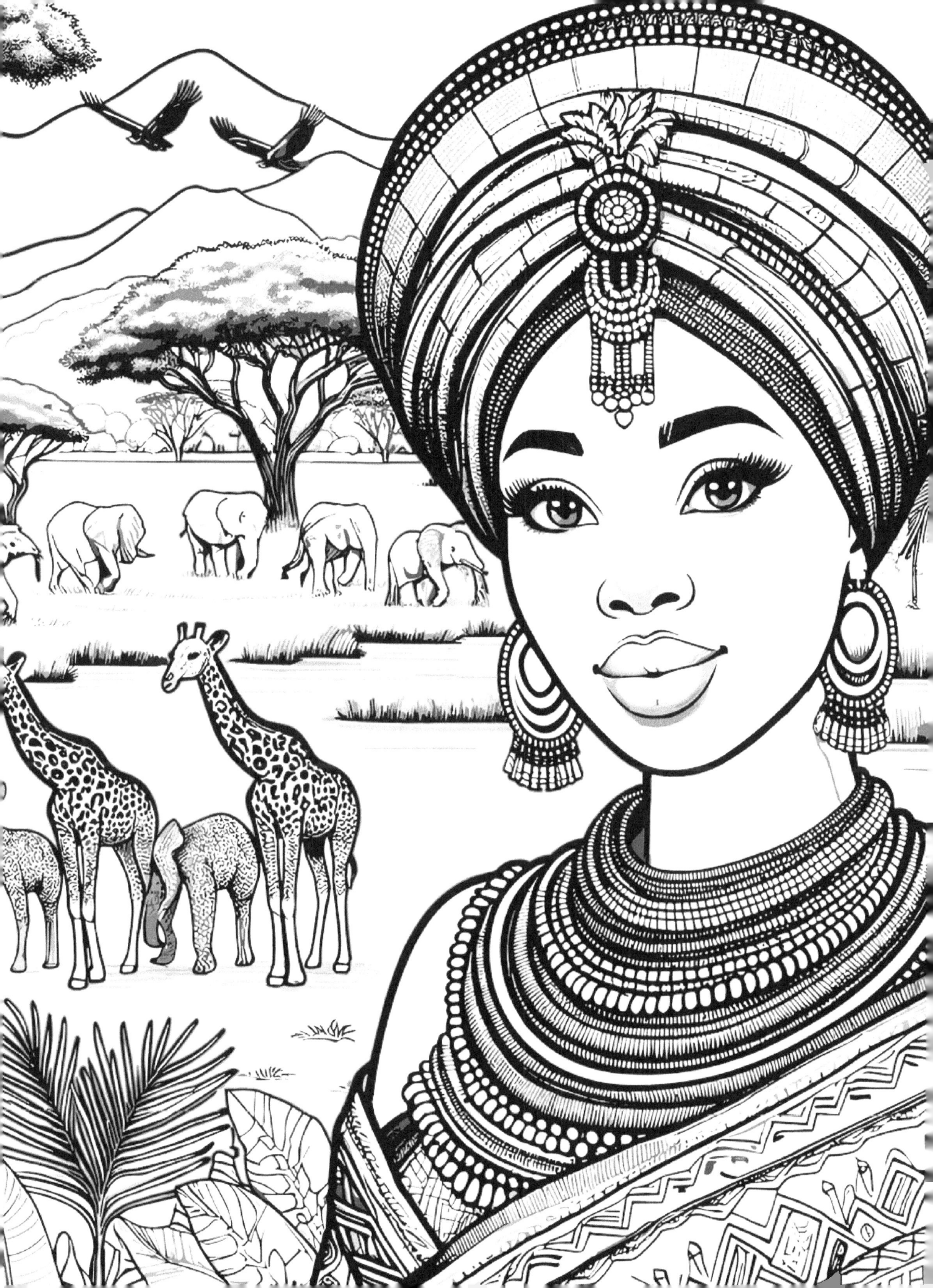

BERBER

(bur·br)

The Berber people live in the countries of North Africa, like Morocco, Algeria, and Egypt.

They have lived there for a very, very long time – over 5,000 years!

The Berber speak their own amazing languages and have their own traditions.

A long time ago, the Berber people built villages and cities in the desert.

They traveled in caravans across the Sahara.

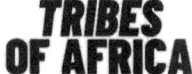

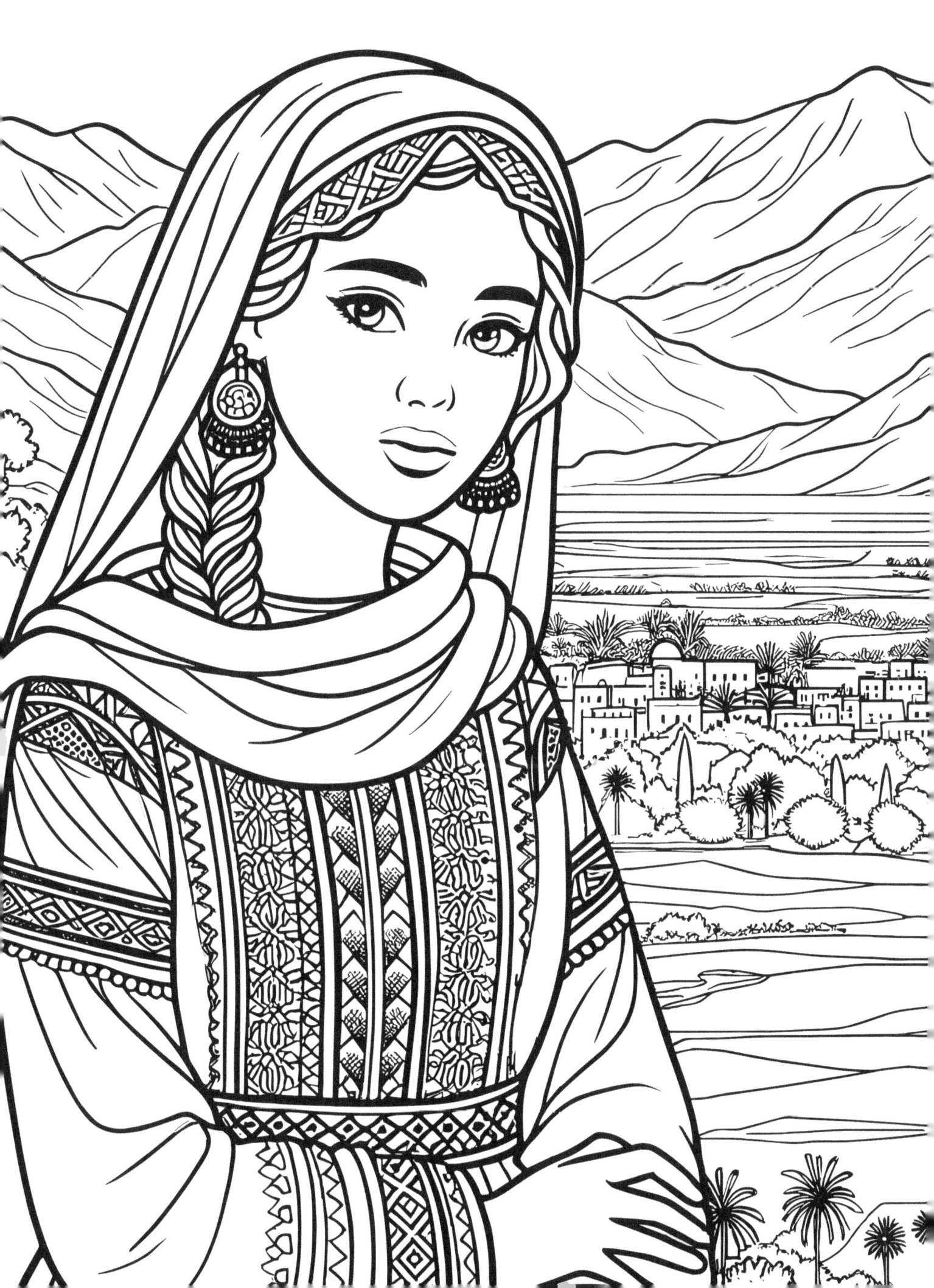

BOA VISTA
(boa·vista)

Cape Verde is a country with a rich and diverse culture, but unlike some other countries, it doesn't have tribes in the traditional sense.

Cape Verdean women are from Cape Verde, a group of islands off the coast of Africa.

Cape Verdean women are very family-oriented. They love to spend time with their families and friends.

Cape Verdean women are very creative. They love to sing, dance, and cook.

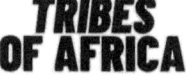

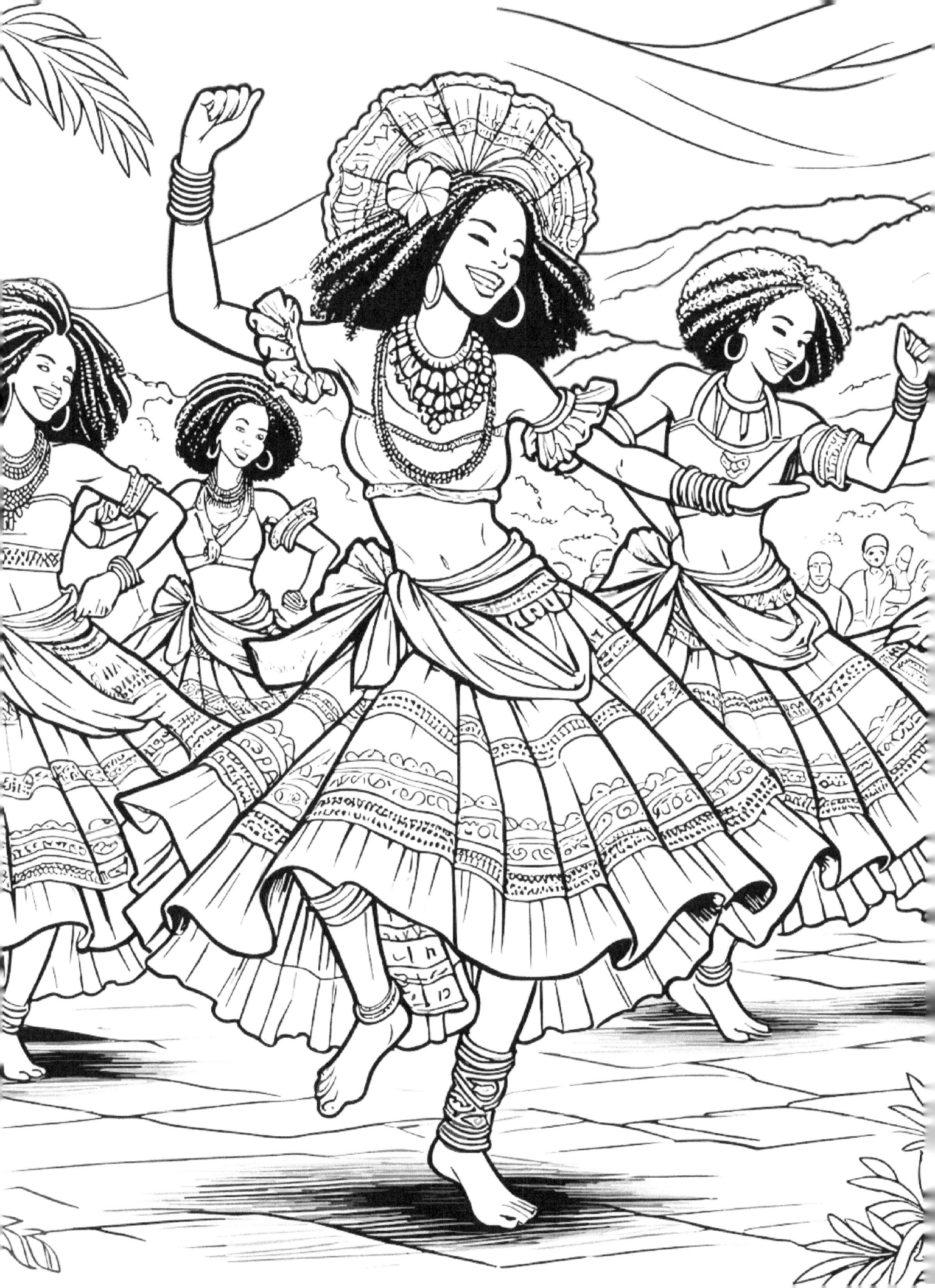

FANTE
(fan·tee)

The Fante are a group of people who live in Ghana in West Africa.

They have lived along the coastal region of Ghana for hundreds of years.

The Fante speak their own language called Fante.

They have their own traditions and culture.

In the past, the Fante had their own kingdom with chiefs and kings.

They traded with Europeans who came on ships.

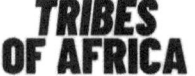

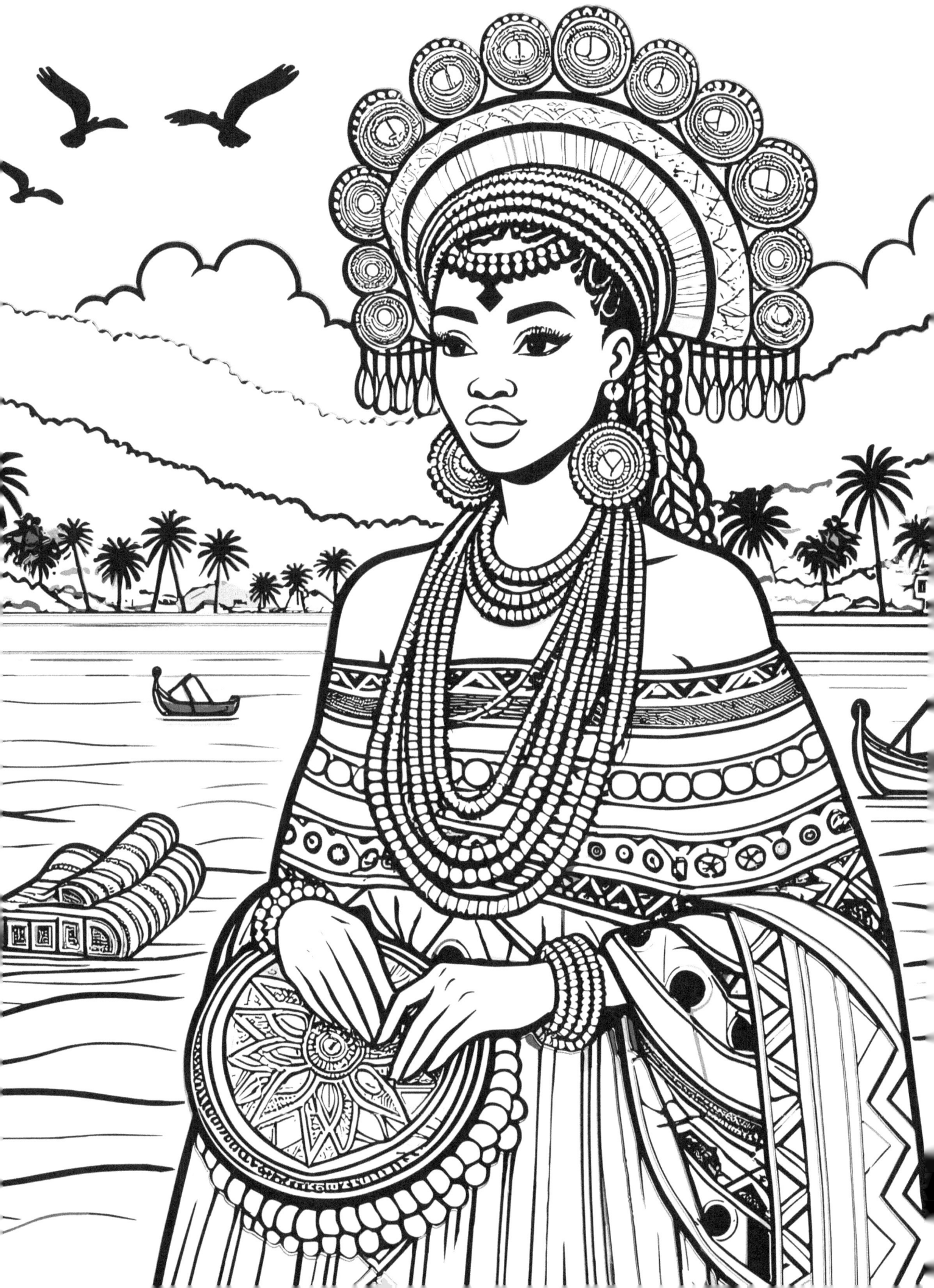

FULANI
(foo·laa·nee)

The Fulani people live in many countries in West Africa and Central Africa.

They have lived in Africa as nomads and settlers for over a thousand years.

The Fulani speak their own language called Fulfulde.

They have their own culture.

In the past, the Fulani established powerful kingdoms and empires in West Africa.

They were fierce warriors and traders.

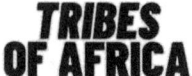

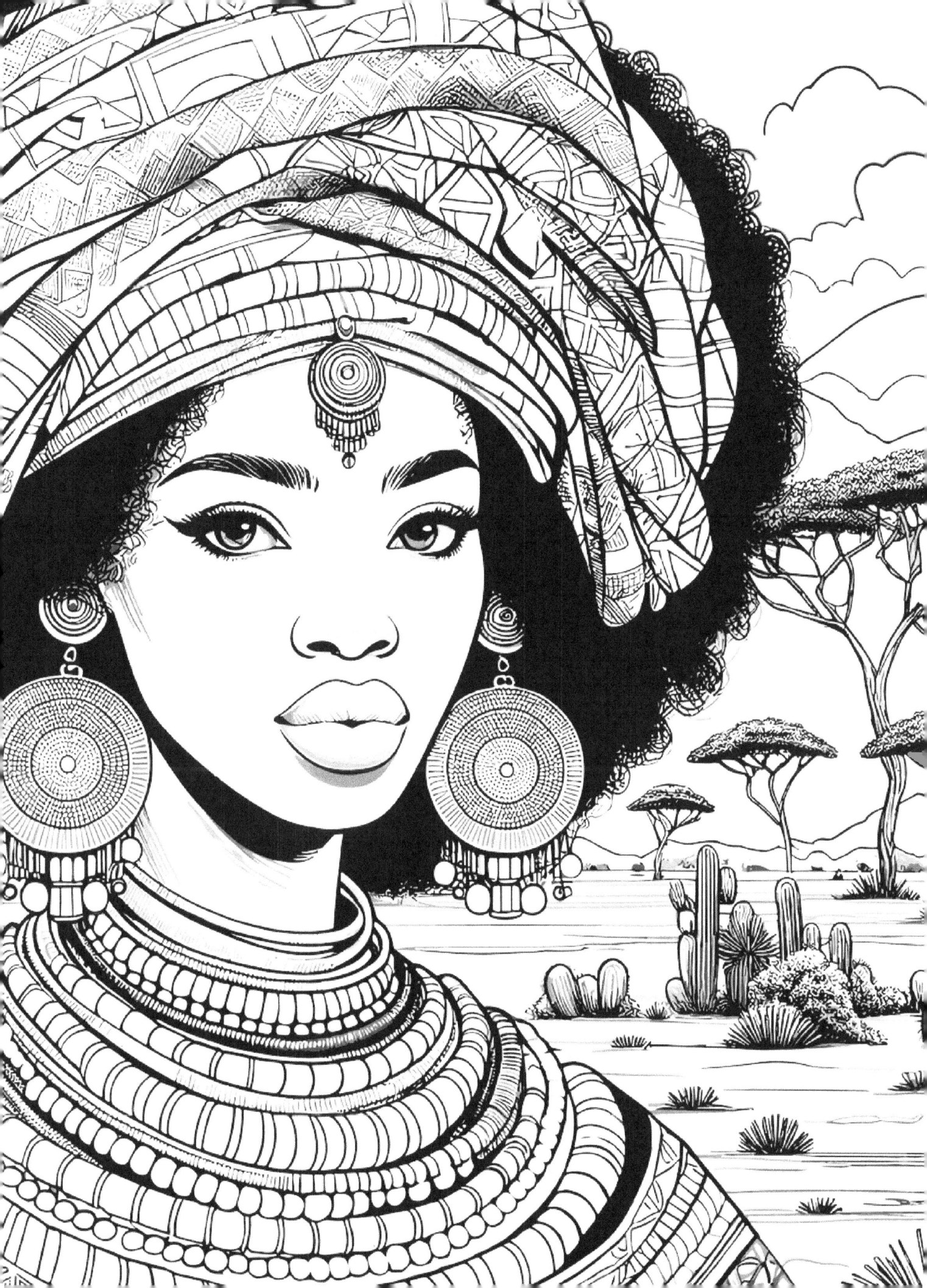

GA

(ga)

The Ga people live in Ghana in West Africa.

They have lived along the coast of Ghana for a very long time.

The Ga speak their own language which is also called Ga.

In the past, the Ga had their own Ga kingdoms near the city of Accra.

They fished along the ocean and traded with other Africans and Europeans.

Later, the Ga fought against British colonizers to defend their lands.

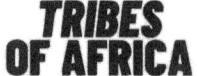

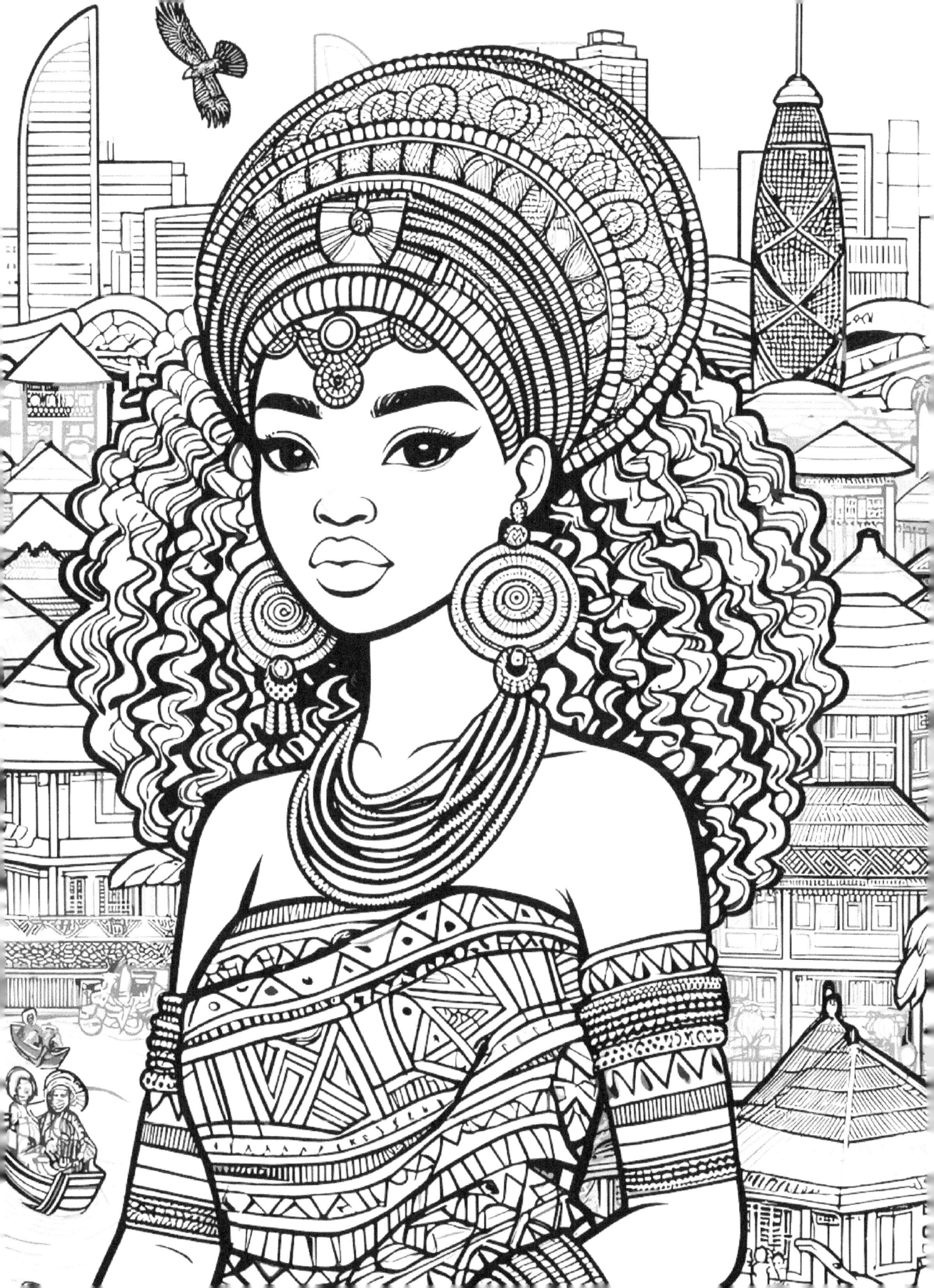

HAUSA
(hau·suh)

The Hausa people live in West Africa in countries like Nigeria and Niger.

They have inhabited the grasslands and savannas of West Africa for over 1,000 years.

The Hausa have their own language called Hausawhich is widely spoken in the region.

Long ago, the Hausa built great ancient kingdoms like Kano, Katsina and Zazzau.

They were powerful traders and warriors.

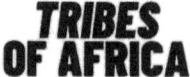

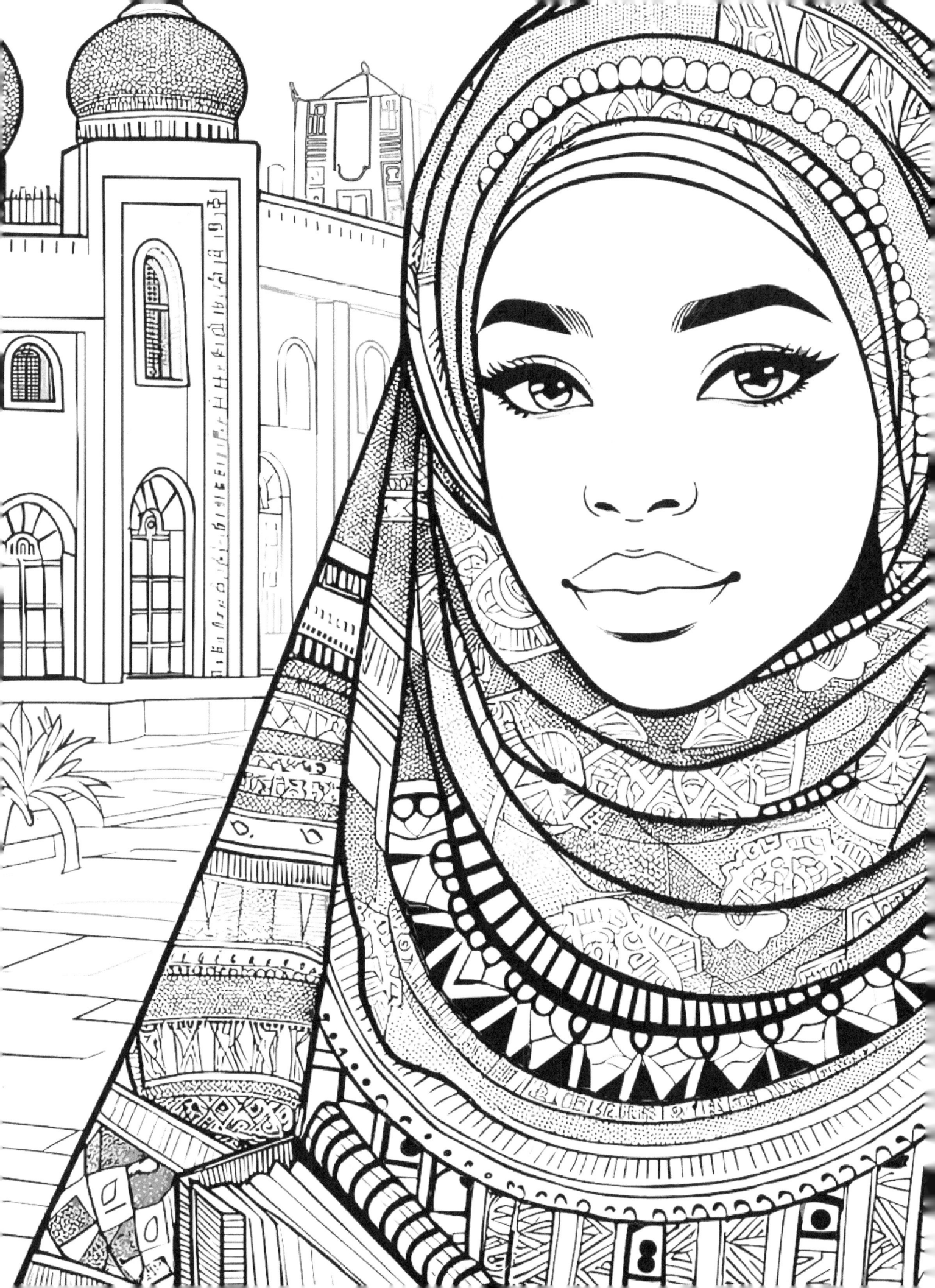

HIMBA

(him·buh)

The Himba are indigenous people who live in northern Namibia in Africa.

They have lived there for many generations, herding and farming.

The Himba have their own language called Otjihimba.

Himba villages are made up of small mud and stick houses.

The Himba are pastoral people, so they raise cows, goats, and sheep.

The animals give them milk, meat, and skins.

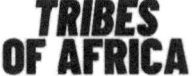

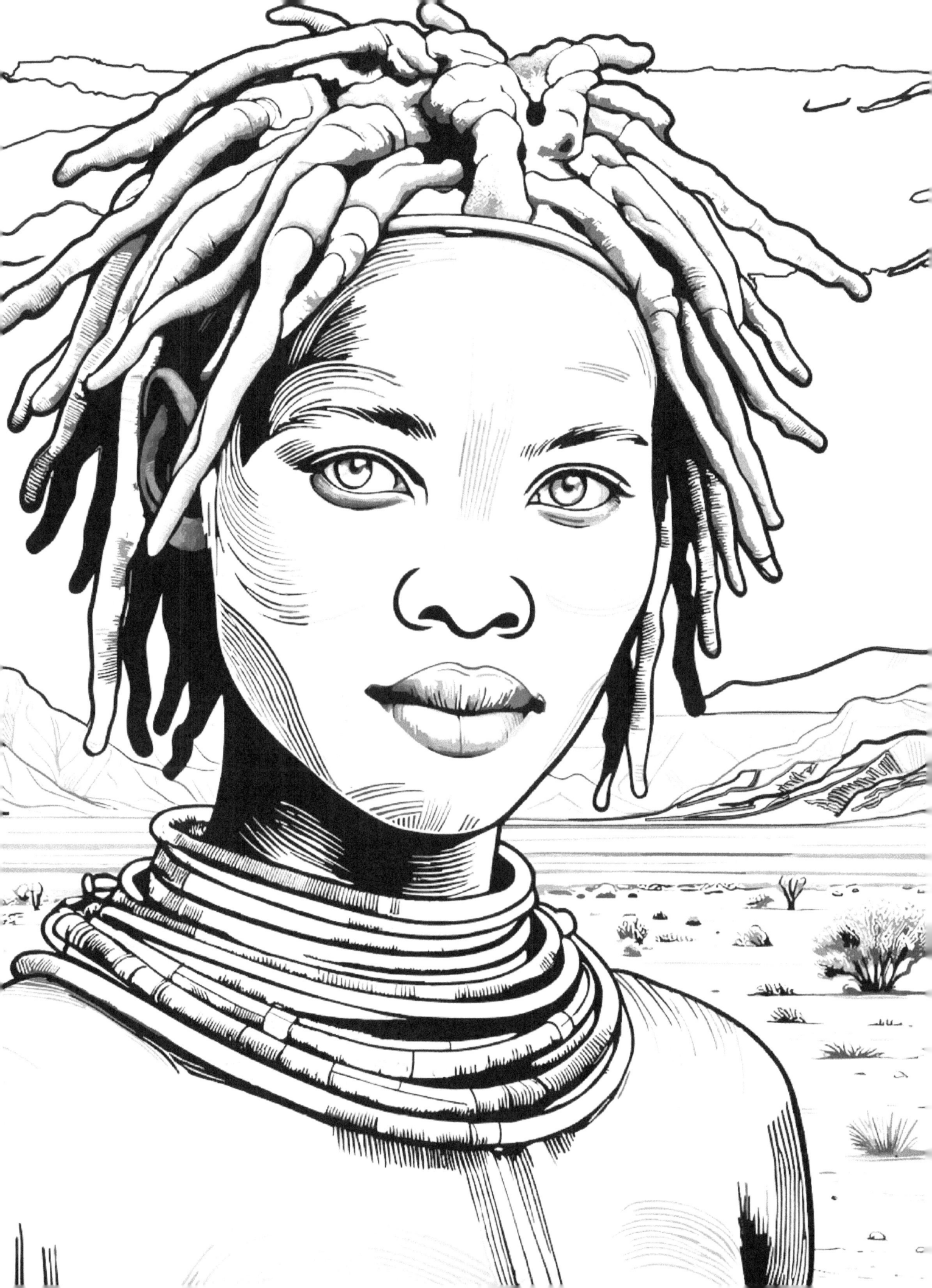

IGBO

(ig·bow)

The Igbo people live in Nigeria in West Africa.

They have lived in southeastern Nigeria for a very long time, for thousands of years.

The Igbo speak their own language also called Igbo.

In the past, the Igbo had different village chiefs instead of kings.

Igbo villagers lived in round mud houses with cone-shaped roofs.

The Igbo were good metal workers and made iron tools and weapons.

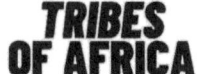

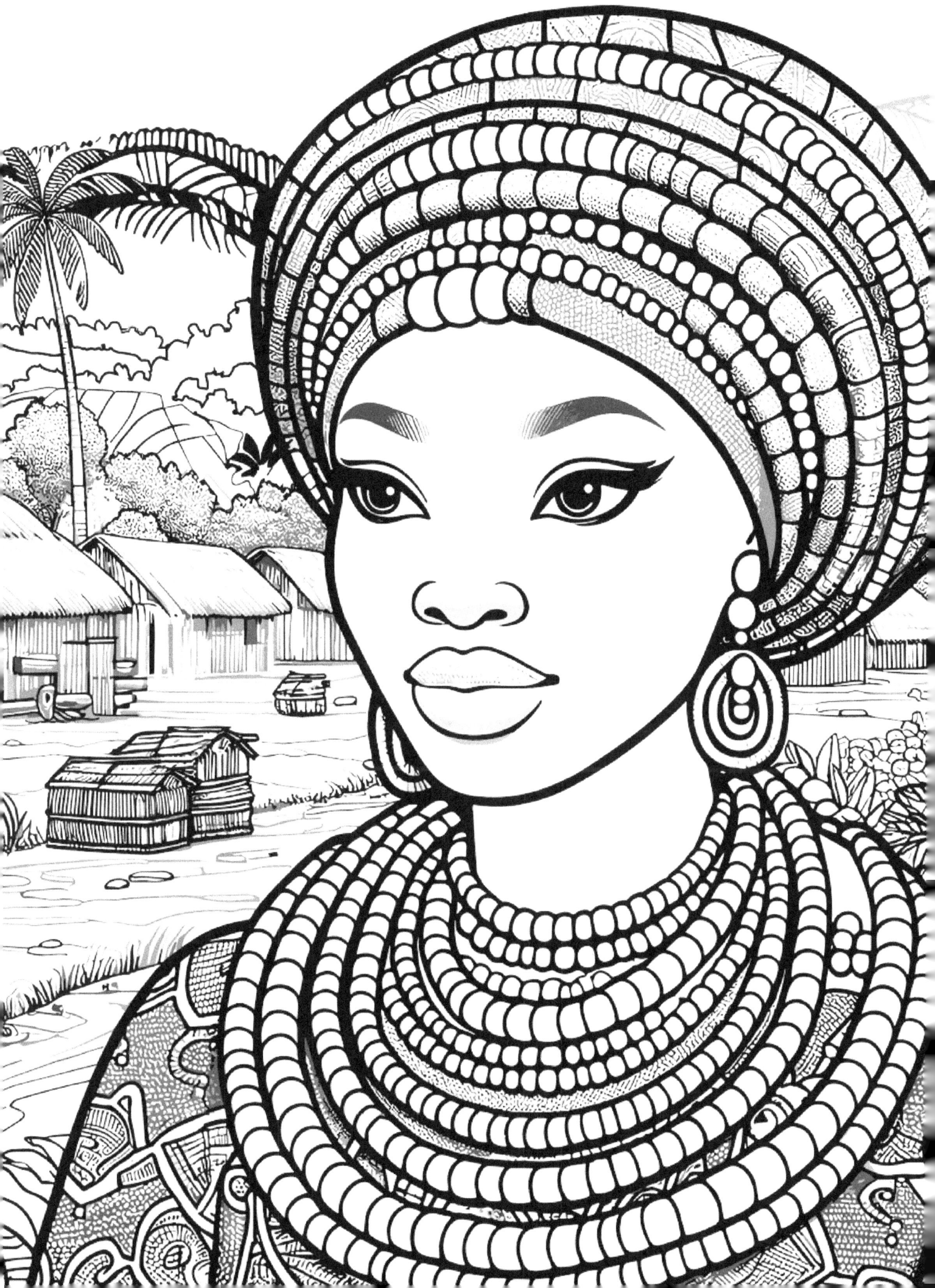

MAASAI
(muh·sai)

The Maasai people live in Kenya and Tanzania in East Africa.

They have lived in these lands for hundreds of years, moving with their cattle.

The Maasai speak their own language called Maa.

In the past, Maasai warriors protected their tribes from enemies.

They were tall and fierce fighters.

The Maasai are pastoral people – their cows, goats and sheep are important to them.

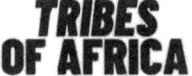

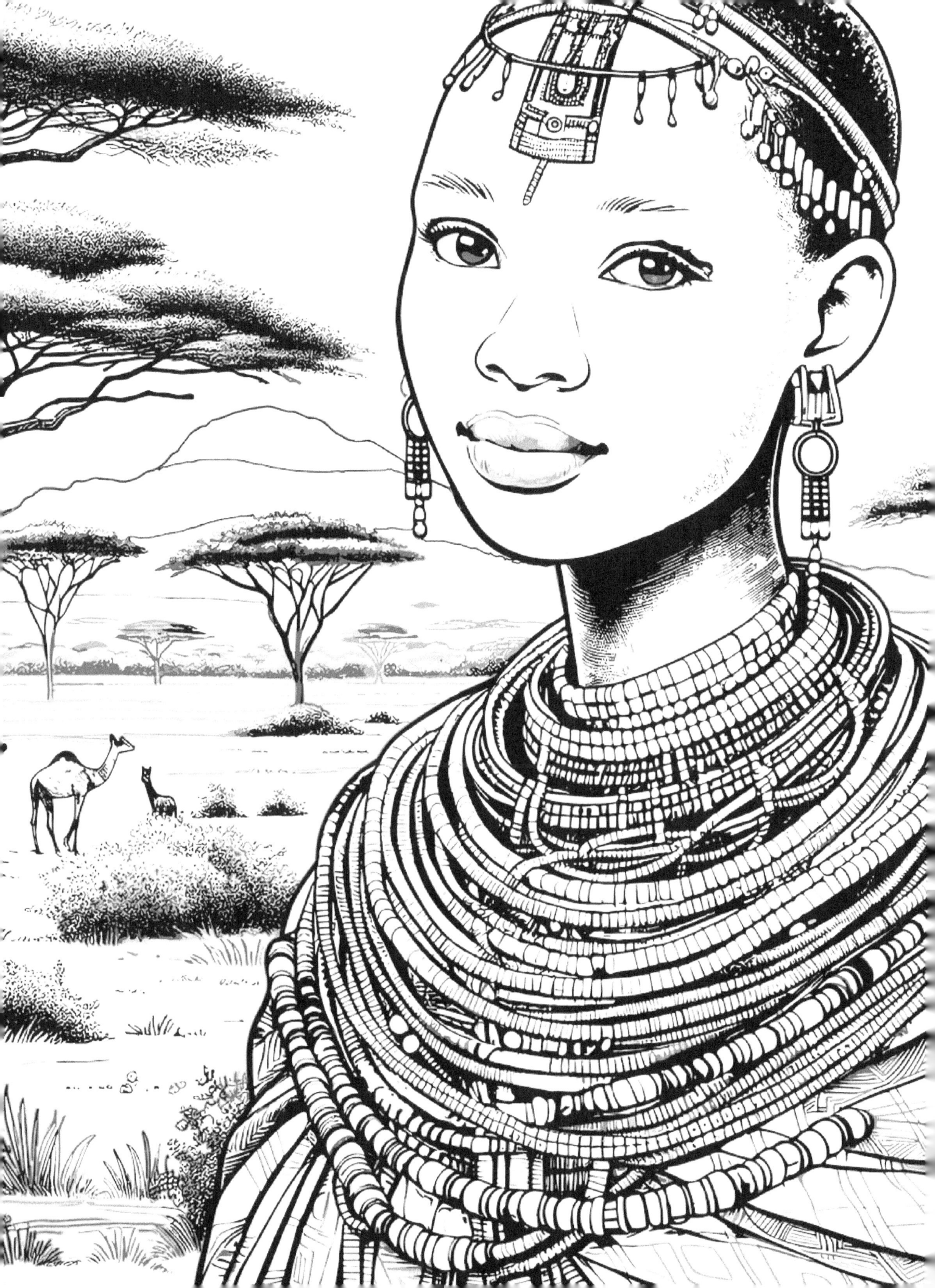

OROMO
(aw·row·mow)

The Oromo people live in the country of Ethiopia in Africa.

The Oromo speak their own language called Oromiffa.

They have their own traditions and culture.

In the past, the Oromo traveled with their animals and lived as nomads in the open countryside.

Today, Oromo make up Ethiopia's largest ethnic group - over 25 million people!

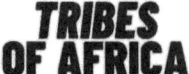

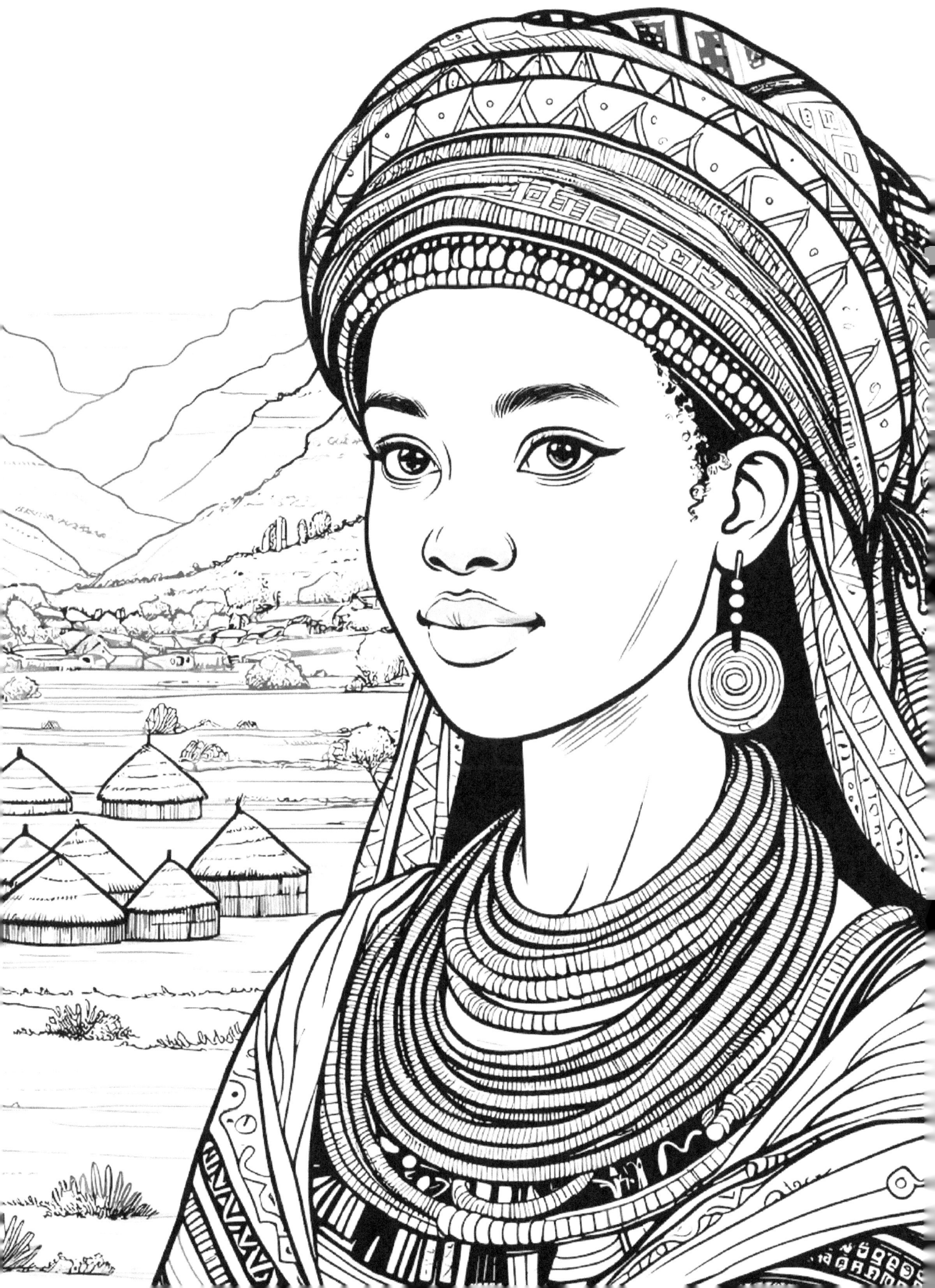

TIGRAY

(tee·gray)

The Tigray are an ethnic group who live in northern Ethiopia in Africa.

They have inhabited this highland region for over 2,000 years!

The Tigray people speak their own language called Tigrinya.

In ancient times, the Tigray had a powerful kingdom called D'mt and Axum with kings and palaces.

They built impressive obelisks, castles and churches out of stone. Some still stand today!

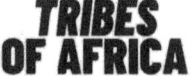

TRIBES OF AFRICA

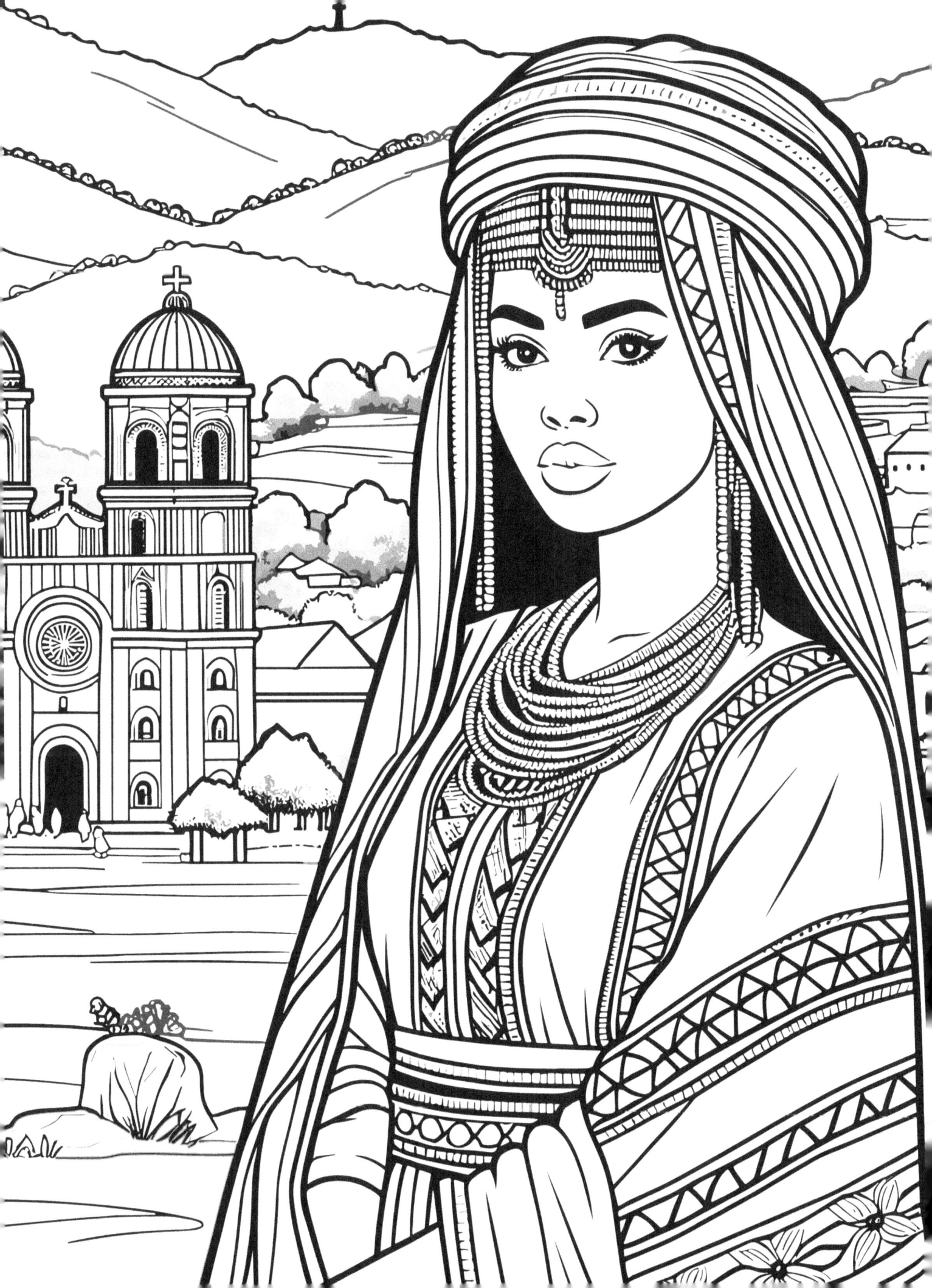

TUAREG
(twaa·reg)

The Tuareg are an indigenous people who live inthe Sahara desert in Africa.

They have lived as nomads in the harsh Sahara for thousands of years!

The Tuareg have their own Amazing language called Tamasheq.

Traditionally, Tuareg were nomadic herders who traveled across the desert with their camels and goats.

The Tuareg women wore veils over their faces and blue indigo clothes to protect them from sun and sand storms.

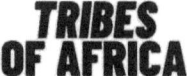

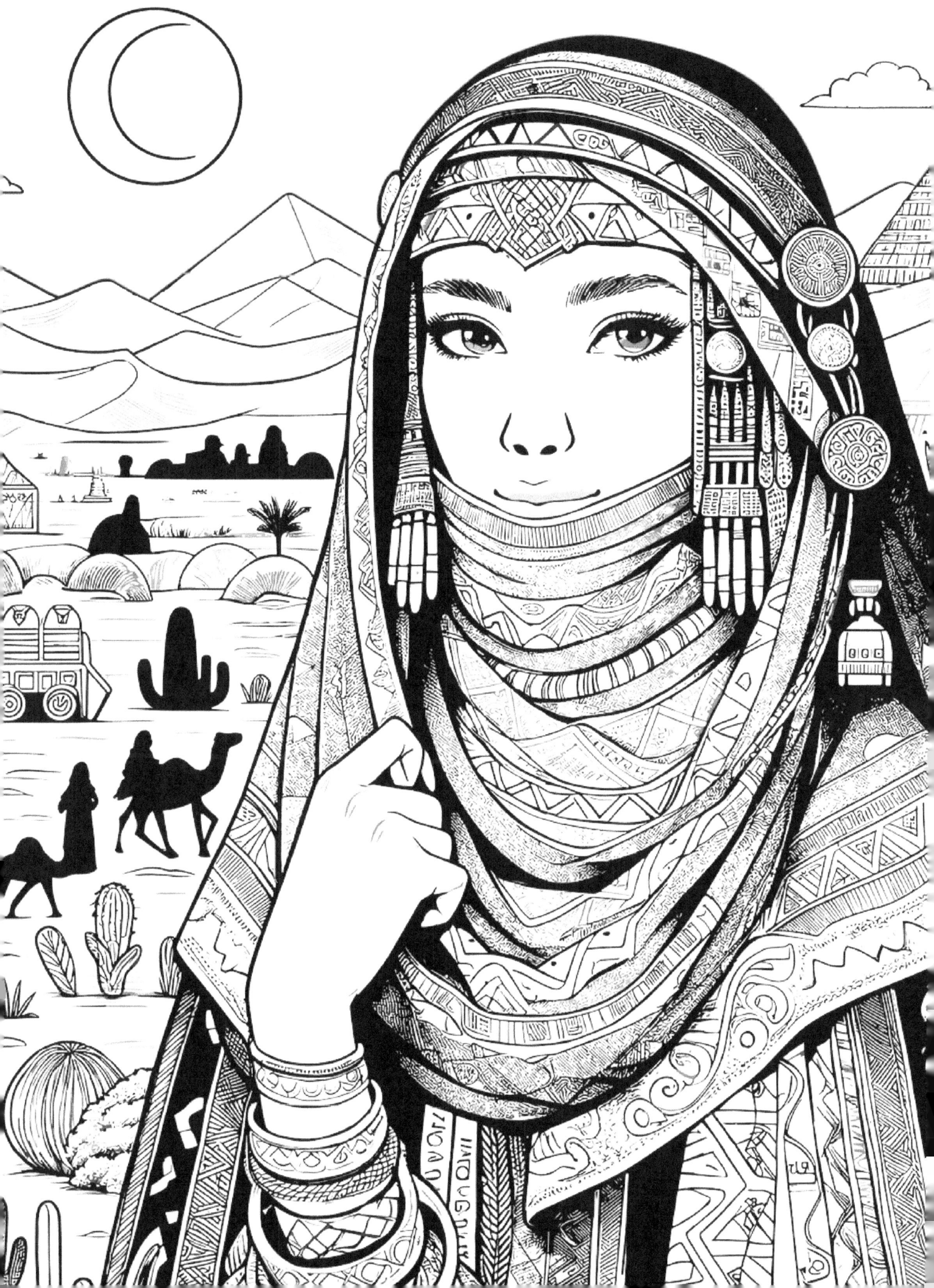

YORUBA

(yaw·roo·buh)

The Yoruba people live in western Nigeria in Africa.

They have lived in this region for thousands of years.

The Yoruba have their own language, also called Yoruba.

In the past, the Yoruba had powerful ancient kingdoms ruled by monarchs called obas.

The Yoruba built large cities and beautiful shrines out of clay and stone.

Yoruba people farmed crops, wove cloth, made iron tools, and created bronze art.

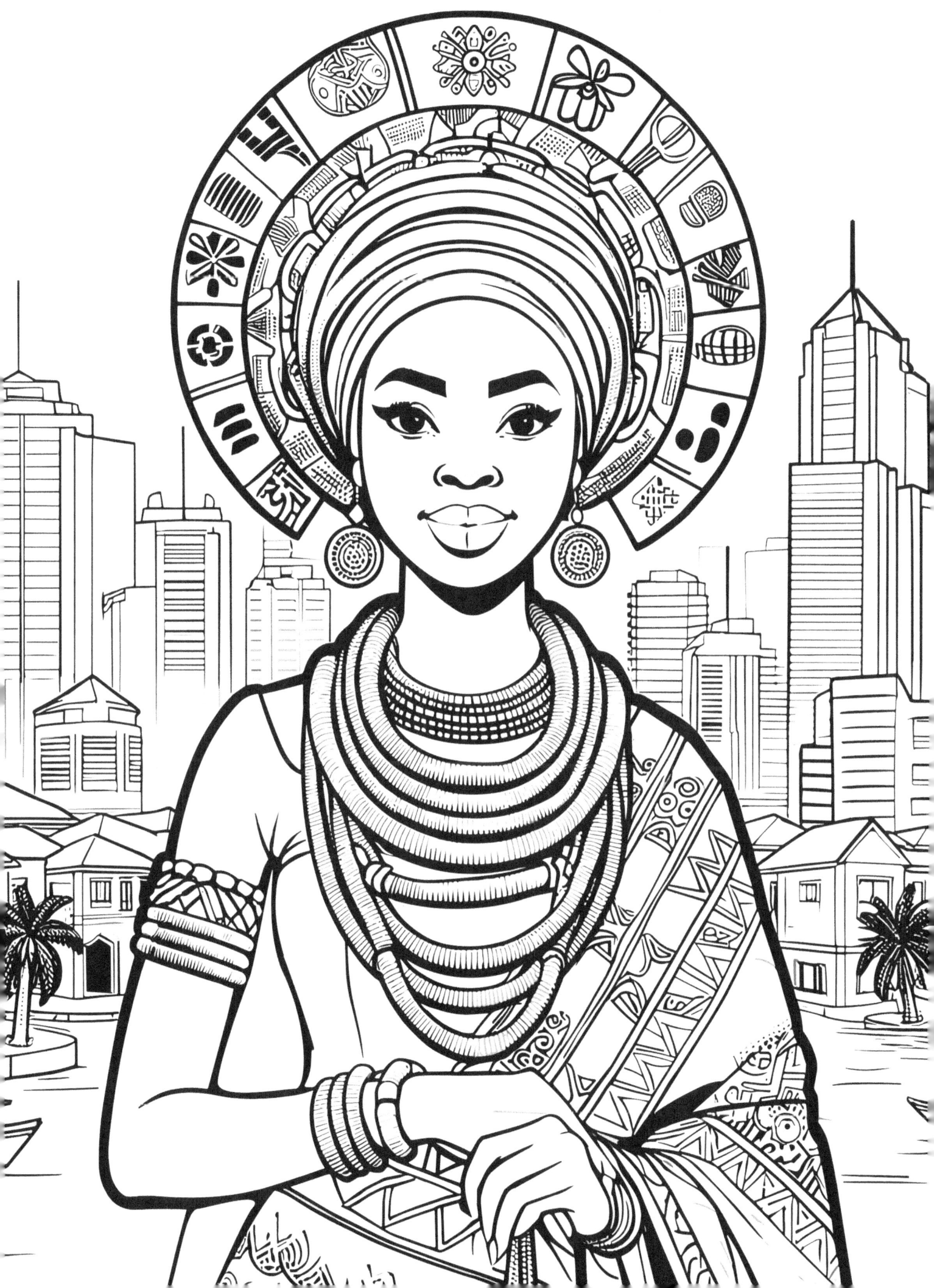

ZULU
(zoo·loo)

The Zulu people live in South Africa in southern Africa.

They have inhabited these lands for hundreds of years.

The Zulu speak their own language called isiZulu.

In the 1800s, a great Zulu king named Shaka Zulu built a huge Zulu empire and army.

Zulu warriors were very fierce fighters who even fought against British invaders with spears.

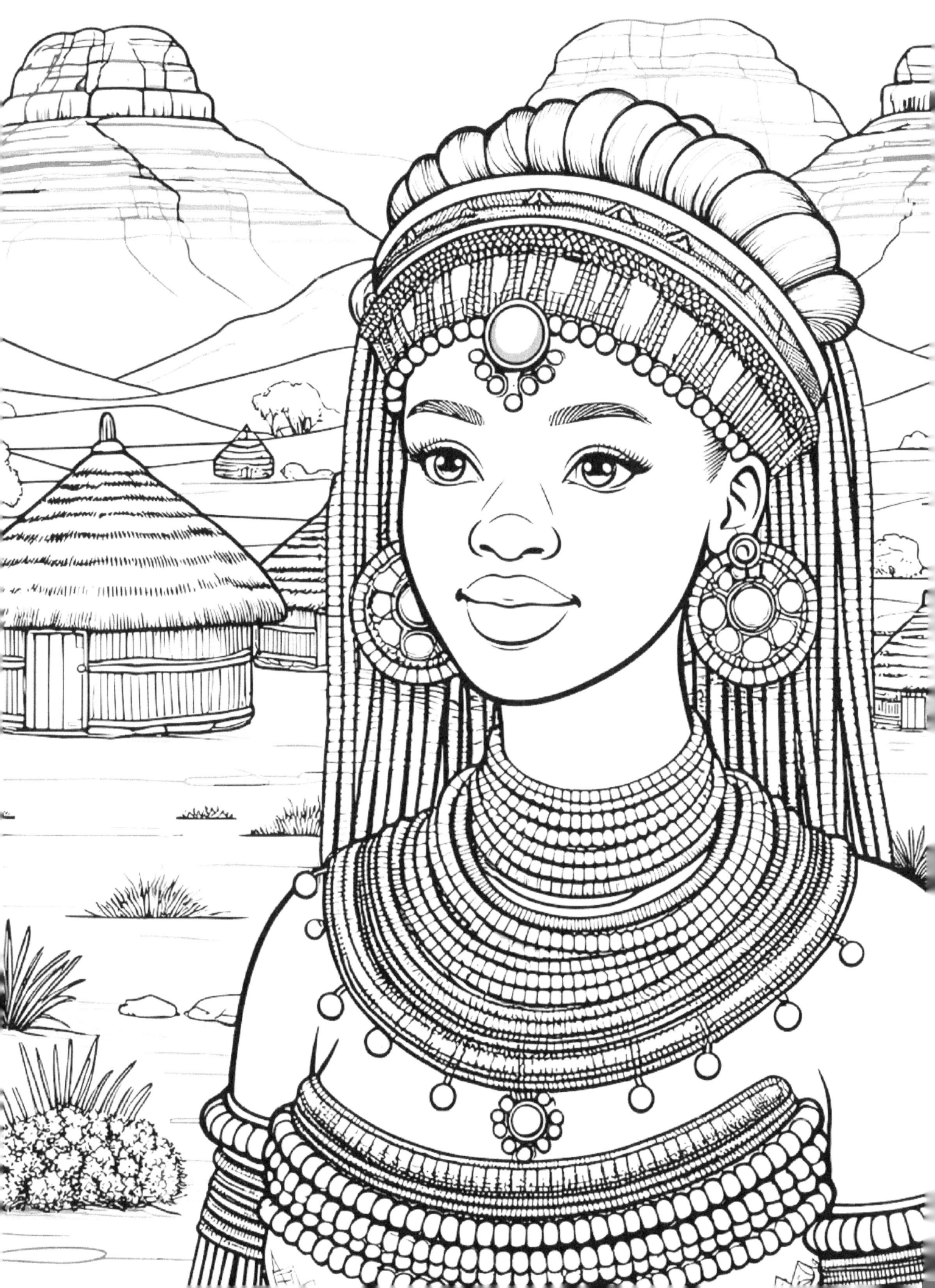

THE END NOTE

Thank you for embarking on this vibrant journey through "Tribes of Africa: Women's Edition." Your coloring has brought to life the diverse cultures and traditions of Africa's tribes, celebrating the strength and spirit of their women.

As we conclude this book, the adventure continues with our "Tribes of Africa Calendar," available at **tribesofafrica.org**. Filled with stunning illustrations and fascinating tribal facts, it serves as the perfect year-round companion to your coloring experience.

Your support contributes to cultural preservation efforts, helping to keep these rich traditions alive. We look forward to your continued exploration and appreciation of Africa's cultural heritage.

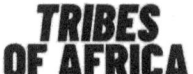

TRIBES
OF AFRICA

Happy coloring and discovery!
Best wishes,

The Tribes of Africa Team

tribesofafrica.org